To **CODY AND MURPHY.**

Although you can't read, you wrote this book.

www.mascotbooks.com

Happy Tails: Lessons From Dogs on How to Live Your Best Life

For more information, please contact:
Mascot Books
620 Herndon Parkway, Suite 320
Herndon, VA 20170
info@mascotbooks.com

Library of Congress Control Number: 2017916225

CPSIA Code: PRTWP1217A
ISBN-13: 978-1-68401-683-9

Printed in Malaysia

Happy Tails

Lessons From Dogs on How to Live Your Best Life

Chris Rathmann

Over time, we dogs have noticed that humans have lost their ability to be in the present moment, find the joy in every experience, and simply have fun. Humans are always in a rush, rarely slowing down to take a nice long walk around the park or through the woods. They don't even stop to smell the grass and the trees, or take a moment to introduce themselves to a stranger. And those annoying beeping and ringing devices they use—it's like they're glued to them! With so much hurrying around, those humans forget what it's like to have fun in the moment. We want them to stop missing out on all the fun!

Fortunately, the solution is lying right at their feet (and sometimes under them).

US DOGS.

So put down the devices, pick up the leashes, and let us teach you a thing or two about enjoying life. You'll soon find joy in the simple wonder and beauty that is all around you.

HAPPY TAILS...

" Be in the moment.
Us dogs don't worry
about what happened
five minutes ago, or
what might happen five
minutes from now. There
is too much fun to be
had, right now! **"**

" **PLAY** with passion. "

" **EAT with passion.** "

" **It's okay...**

...to go a little CRAZY sometimes. "

" **EXERCISE hard!** "

" Rest even harder. "

" **ALWAYS** shake hands and look people in the eyes. "

" **If you discriminate or pre-judge, you may miss out on making a new BEST friend.** "

" Say please. "

" **And thank you.** "

"Take long walks and connect with nature."

" When hard times come; shake it off. "

" Stop to enjoy the sights and smells. "

" **UNLEASH** your talents. "

" Learn new things, at ANY age. "

"Be compassionate to those who are in need."

" **If you have a little extra,** **it's okay to share.** "

" BE BRAVE.
Conquer your
fears. "

"CHASE your dreams, no matter how big or small. Don't let the fear of failure stop you from trying."

" Be proud of who you are. "

"Always let those you love know that you love them."

" And always lead with a smile...
and a wag. "

CHRIS RATHMANN IS OUR DAD.

He isn't an authority on dogs or a famous author (yet), but he sure knows how to love a dog and how to make our tails wag. He says we make his heart warm, and that is what he is hoping to do for others by sharing some of the lessons we have taught him.

Thanks for reading his book.

His beloved companions,

Cody and Murphy Rathmann

Have a book idea?
Contact us at:

info@mascotbooks.com | www.mascotbooks.com